£5.99

R10864

THE BOY FILES

THE BOY FILES

FILES

Puberty, growing up and all THAT stuff

ALEX HOOPER-HODSON

WAYLAND

Dedicated to my wonderful partner Morella for all the cups of
coffee she made me. Thanks to Phillip & Anne for their proof
reading skills. And to 10 year old Luke who played the part of
my target audience.

First published in 2013 by Wayland
Copyright © Wayland 2013
Wayland
338 Euston Road
London NW1 3BH

Wayland Australia
Level 17/207 Kent Street
Sydney NSW 2000

Editor: Nicola Edwards
Design: Simon Daley, Giraffe

British Library Cataloguing in Publication Data
Hooper-Hodson, Alex.
  Boy files : puberty, growing up and all that stuff.
  1. Boys--Health and hygiene--Juvenile literature.
  2. Puberty--Juvenile literature. 3. Boys--Life skills
  guides--Juvenile literature.
  I. Title

  305.2'3'0811-dc23
ISBN: 978 0 7502 7770 9

Printed in China

10 9 8 7 6 5 4 3 2

Wayland is a division of Hachette Children's Books,
an Hachette UK company
www.hachette.co.uk

Contents

Welcome to THE BOY FILES

Hi!

The book you hold in your hand is no ordinary book. It's a personal dossier, full of facts you'll need to know about things that could or will happen to you in the near future. **Changes are going to take place in your body** and in your mind, and you are going to transform (yes, like Optimus Prime) into somebody different. This transformation has a name; it's called puberty. Knowing about puberty before it happens to you can help stop you feeling lost and confused – and that's where I come in.

THE BOY FILES was written by me, Alex Hooper-Hodson, to be your guide through this difficult period. Think of it like a **walkthrough** for your **favourite X-Box game**. It has all the maps and secrets and can even help you cheat a little. I'm hoping that some of the experience I've gained helping young people in my magazine and newspaper columns will rub off on you. I've included some real-life problems that were sent to me to show that **you really aren't going through this alone** and to give you an insight into the worries some people encounter during this often troubled time.

Puberty is a serious subject but this book is also about **fun** and I promise not to send you to sleep. So sit back, relax, and prepare to have your brain squeezed like a giant lemon as you discover the amazing truth about your own body.

CHAPTER 1

Even superheroes
go through puberty

All this talk of your body changing can sound really scary, but it's important for you to understand that everyone goes through puberty, and I mean **EVERYONE**! Your dad went through puberty and he's alright, isn't he? Your big brother did too, and I bet he makes the most out of being bigger and stronger than you. The entire England football team went through puberty, which is why they have the speed and strength to score those winning goals (sometimes). Even superheroes like Batman and Superman went through puberty.

The point is, although the things I tell you about will sound new and scary, they're really **natural** and **necessary**. Never fear! **THE BOY FILES** will have the answers to all your questions, queries, worries and wonders. It's also really important that you don't start to worry if the things I talk about haven't affected you yet. Puberty happens at different times to different people – we all change at different rates! This is nothing to be ashamed of or to feel bad about.

Going through puberty is something you should feel proud of, but I don't want you to get hung up waiting for it to happen. And when puberty comes knocking, **DON'T PANIC**! This book is here to help you. It doesn't have the power to put things back to the way they were before but it can help you to adjust to the changes and understand what is happening to you.

So what kind of changes should you come to expect? From what you've read so far I wouldn't blame you for thinking you might be about to turn into some kind of futuristic transforming robot. Whilst puberty isn't **THAT** exciting, there's nothing wrong with thinking about it in a fun kind of way. Rather than seeing puberty as a terrible ordeal which Mother Nature forces you to endure, why not imagine you're a superhero and that puberty is your origin story, the fantastical process by which you get your **SUPERPOWERS**.

You will gain new strength because puberty makes your muscles start to develop and grow. You may find that for a while you have a sort of 'sonic scream' while your voice breaks, which is when it changes from being high and squeaky (like it is now!) and becomes deeper and more throaty.

You could find that you have heightened emotions for a few years but there's no harm in thinking of these as 'psychic senses' such as Professor X might have.

You may even find you get the power of super-size as you go through **growth spurts**, which make you grow much taller in a short space of time. What's important to realise is that puberty is nature's way of upgrading your body to prepare you for manhood rather than some sort of punishment or disease.

What's happening to me?

Here is a list of the main changes you should expect to experience as you get a bit older:

- Your height and weight will increase.

- Hair will start to grow in the pubic area (around your willy), under your arms, on your face and on your legs.

- Your muscles will get stronger and more defined.

- Your vocal chords will get thicker and longer, and your voice will break.

- You will start to find you sweat more as sweat and oil glands become more active. If you don't wash this sweat away regularly it will start to smell. People call this 'BO' (body odour).

- Spots (also called zits, pimples or acne) can develop, due to your increasingly oily skin. Unfortunately some people get lots of these.

- Your willy (or penis, to use the official terminology) will get bigger and you will start to have erections and may begin to produce sperm in the form of 'wet dreams'.

- You will start to look at girls differently...

The puberty alphabet

Here is an A-Z with a difference – The Puberty Alphabet, designed to give you a quick reference guide to some of the fantastic facts we'll be discussing in later chapters.

A is for **Armpit Hair:** During puberty you'll notice hair start to appear in new places, particularly under your arms.

B is for **Bad Breath**: You might be tempted to skip brushing your teeth in the morning, but if you do don't be surprised if your friends turn green and back away when you talk to them!

C is for **Changes**: Your body will undergo some major changes but with this guide you'll know what to expect and how to handle them.

D is for **Differences**: You'll notice the differences between boys and girls as you get older. For now it's important to know that girls' puberty isn't identical to boys'.

E is for **Embarrassing Erections**: You're going to find that your willy has a mind of its own. Erections can happen out of the blue and at the worst possible time!

F is for **Finishing School**: Leaving primary school can be a shock to the system, but it's a new stage of life and a chance to make more friends.

G is for **Growth Spurts**: You won't become a giant overnight, but you might find you grow very quickly and at unpredictable intervals.

H is for **Hormones**: Testosterone triggers the major changes of puberty and it can also influence your behaviour.

I is for **Increased Appetite**: All that growing means your body's going to need more fuel. By eating healthily you'll grow in all the right ways.

J is **Jealousy**: Your mates might develop faster than you. They might also boast about their sex lives (although most of the time they'll be lying!). Don't get jealous, because puberty affects us at different rates.

K is for **Keeping Safe**: This includes everything from walking down the street to using social networking sites online.

L is for **Late Development**: Some boys don't start puberty until they are 14 or 15. If you are worried that puberty is never going to happen to you, your doctor will be able to reassure you.

M is for **Mood Swings**: As your hormones kick in they can make your emotions go up and down like a runaway rollercoaster. It helps to manage your moods if you understand what's happening to you.

N is for **Nutrition**: Part of growing big and strong involves eating the right things so that your body gets the nutrients it needs to grow.

O is for **Oversleeping**: One of the big changes you'll begin to notice is how much more sleep you need. Getting to bed early is the best way to cope!

P is for **Puberty**: No puberty alphabet would be complete without a mention of the P word. Puberty can start from the age of 9 and is what turns you from a boy into a man.

Q is for **Questions**: You're bound to have a ton of questions about puberty. In these pages you'll find case studies, real life problems and SOLVE IT boxes which will give you the answers you need.

R is **Rules (Breaking them)**: As you get older and want more independence you may start to question all the rules laid down by adults. Some rules are there for excellent reasons – and I'll explain why it's important for you stick to these in a later chapter.

S is for **Sweat**: Along with your new hairy armpits comes super-stinky sweat. Make sure you wash regularly and use deodorant.

T is for **Talking**: Don't keep things bottled up! Puberty can give you a lot to talk about and it's best to ask questions and to let adults know when you're concerned about something.

U is for the **Unexpected**: It's what puberty is all about. The changes you are reading about can happen at the worst possible time or when you least anticipate them.

V is for **Voice**: Over the next few years your vocal chords will grow thicker and longer and your voice will get deeper. There may a short period when it sounds scratchy and high-pitched. This is known as your voice 'breaking'.

W is for **Willy Worries**: All lads worry about their willies at some stage. It's totally normal to think that yours might be the wrong size or shape. If your mates tell you that they've got a huge one don't be concerned – 99% of the time they'll be fibbing!

X is for **X-Factor**: No, I don't mean the TV show. If you want people to see your X-factor, read the chapter on body confidence.

Y is for **You**: It's what this book is all about! Read on to find out what the future has in store for YOU!

Z is for **Zits**: Those red, painful pustules that appear on your face. Zits can be a nightmare when you're going through puberty, but there are ways to manage your acne and we'll discuss them later in the book.

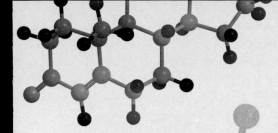

All about hormones

What they are and what they do – everything from restless legs to bad moods.

You may have heard grown-ups talking about their 'hormones'. Sometimes women complain that hormones make them feel excited or **moody**. Well, men have hormones too. Don't worry if you don't yet know what a 'hormone' is because I'm going to tell you, but it's more important to understand what hormones do and how they affect you rather than what they are.

Information carriers

It's hard to imagine what hormones look like because they're really just chemicals being produced inside your body by things called glands. Think of hormones as little **messengers** that carry **super-important information** from one part of your body to another. They can tell your body all sorts of things, such as when it's hot and you need to sweat to cool down, when it's time to go to sleep or when to be hungry so that you take in food to give you energy. Very importantly, there are certain hormones that are produced when your body is ready to go through the **BIG CHANGES** of puberty.

An essential hormone...

In the case of boys and puberty the hormone to know about is **TESTOSTERONE**, or the male sex hormone. When we reach a certain age (which is slightly different for each of us) our glands start producing testosterone. It has the effect of making us 'more male'. All the things you associate with your favourite WWF wrestlers come from testosterone: big muscles, deep voice, hairy arms and chest and beards and moustaches.

... And its unwelcome side-effects

Although it's vital to puberty, testosterone can trigger some side-effects that might bother you and those around you. It can help to be aware of them so you know why you may suddenly be behaving in ways you aren't used to.

Hormones can make you experience extremes of emotions. One minute you might be on top of the world, and then suddenly find yourself sinking into a pit of despair. Your hormones can make you get furious about things you don't normally care about or really sad over the smallest thing. They can give you 'restless legs' that constantly jiggle up and down (much to the irritation of anyone sitting next to you on the sofa!) or make you so sleepy that you stay in bed for 12 hours at a time.

Really, the presence of these side-effects shows you that puberty is all going to plan, and my advice is to work with them rather than against them. If you feel down for no particular reason or want to scream at your parents, tell yourself "it's just the hormones". When you feel really tired, try going to bed a little earlier. Your body is telling you it needs more sleep so it can work on gradually changing you into an adult.

Puberty begins...

Puberty can begin at any age between nine and 14, or sometimes even later. Most of the major changes take place within about four years. In some cases they can happen in quick succession and the whole process can be over in just a couple of years.

It's different for girls

Girls enter puberty a bit earlier than boys, which is why some of the girls you know may already be starting to change. Girls mature faster than boys, because their bodies have to change even more drastically than boys' (in order one day to make babies) and this is Mother Nature's way of giving them a head start. If you are interested in reading more about girls' puberty, **THE GIRL FILES** has all the information you'll need.

The first signs

The timescale for puberty can change from boy to boy, but the events themselves do follow a specific order. The first thing you might notice is that your scrotum (or balls) has got **larger** and you may have experienced some reddening around this area. This normally occurs about the same time as you get your first pubic hair. At first there will only be a few very soft and almost invisible hairs just above the base of your penis. In time this hair will grow thicker and more wiry and will surround your penis and scrotum.

Size doesn't matter

You may also notice that your willy is getting longer and thicker. Lads have always teased each other about penis size and they always will. Just remember these two facts: the average length of the erect penis is under six inches (about 14 centimetres) and nearly every size of penis works properly and causes no problems.

You may have heard other lads at school mention wet dreams – they're talking about another of the key signs that puberty has kicked off.

Changes

As your penis and scrotum are increasing in size and growing, **invisible changes** happen inside them. One of these is that your scrotum begins to produce sperm. Sperm is what men contribute to the process of making babies, because when a single sperm fuses with a woman's egg it leads to pregnancy.

For a man to help make a baby, he first needs to get what's called an erection, so his body **pumps** blood into his penis to make it larger and harder. Then the man can have sex with the woman and transfer his sperm into her body through a process called ejaculation.

Sperm live in your testicles. When you have a wet dream they mix with other fluid to produce a substance called semen. A wet dream occurs when you ejaculate semen while you're asleep. It may all sound a bit icky and it does take some getting used to, but it's perfectly natural.

Don't worry

The first time you have a wet dream can be distressing, but there is nothing to be scared of. Wet dreams can have **no bad effects** except to make a cold patch in the bed. However, many lads have ejaculated for the first time whilst doing completely different activities, like travelling on a bus or playing an Xbox game. It can happen with little or no stimulation to the penis and is a sign that your body is ready to begin making babies, although it's best to hang on for at least a few more years before you try!

SOLVE IT!

Keep your privates private

It can be embarrassing when your mum and dad start to ask about the details of the changes you're going through in puberty. It's great to be able to talk to them if you have a problem but the sorts of changes we've just been discussing are very personal ones. Now may be the time to ask if you can have a small bolt put on your bedroom door and the bathroom (if there isn't one already). Hopefully your parents will understand that now you're a young man you need your personal space and privacy and will agree to your request.

If they don't like the idea of you locking yourself in ask them nicely if from now on they'll knock before coming into your bedroom or the bathroom when you're in there. There's nothing wrong with wanting to keep these sorts of private changes to yourself and the desire to do so is just another sign you are growing up!

CHAPTER 2

Zits, bits & stinky pits

Becoming body confident

Dear Alex,

Ever since I turned 14 I've had really bad acne. Lots of lads at school have a few spots but I have them all over my face like a rash. I get teased all the time with names like 'pizza face' and 'spotty'. I'm getting so upset that I skip school whenever I can and have got into trouble with my teachers. My parents don't seem to understand and keep telling me it's just a phase and to 'soldier on through it'. I need a practical solution to get my zits under control.

Jason, 14

Most teenagers will find they get the occasional outbreak of spots as their hormones cause a stir at puberty. For some, like Jason, the spread of these spots can get **out of control** and have a serious effect on their self-esteem.

Jason's parents' suggestion to 'soldier on through it' is certainly one way to deal with things, but doesn't provide him with an immediate answer. Whilst it's true that everyone grows out of acne eventually, as we'll see, there are methods of treating it other than suffering in silence.

What causes spots?

Your skin is covered in tiny holes called pores, out of which hairs grow. The hairs are made by tiny organs under the skin called hair follicles. Pores and hair follicles produce sebum, a substance that protects the skin and stops it drying out. During puberty the hair follicles increase the production of sebum and this can **overload the pores** in your skin and end up blocking them.

When a pore is blocked, normal skin bacteria can no longer escape. As the build-up of bacteria increases it causes an infection, which is what creates the pus inside the white head of a spot. The build up of pus can be extremely painful which is why it is always so tempting to 'pop' or 'squeeze' a spot. Although **squeezing** can cause relief it can also damage the surface of your skin, cause scarring and drive the infection deeper into the pore, making things worse.

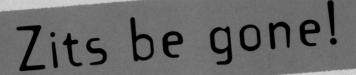

Zits be gone!

Spot remedies that ACTUALLY WORK!

Now you know a bit more about zits it's time to talk about ways to zap them. If you suffer from mild acne a visit to the pharmacist is your best bet for clearer skin and I'm going to give you a super-useful way to know which spot treatment to choose.

Look for treatments that contain a chemical called benzoyl peroxide – **it really works**. It can come in the form of creams you rub in, pads which help exfoliate (open up) the pores, or a face wash you can use every morning. Your pharmacist can advise you what strength is appropriate for you.

Another excellent way to improve the condition of your skin is to *wash your face* twice a day. This, coupled with a healthy diet, can really help to prevent spots. Over-washing can cause the skin to dry out, though, so try not to get carried away.

If you've tried benzoyl peroxide and feel the condition of your skin is still getting worse, it's time to ask Mum or Dad to take you to see your doctor (or GP as they're known). GPs can prescribe treatments that are **much more powerful** than those available over the counter in the pharmacy if they think you need them.

One last piece of advice. If you *are* going to squeeze your spots remember:

- **Clean your hands before you squeeze – there's enough bacteria in there already!**
- **Only squeeze the pimples that have a white head.**
- **Squeeze gently. If it doesn't pop, stop!**

Keeping clean with a morning regime

What is a morning regime? Quite simply it's the routine you carry out every morning, and I mean EVERY morning. Washing is not 'optional'. No one wants a mate who **smells** of stale sweat, **BO** and has **crusty skin** and **greasy hair**. It might sound harsh but can you blame them? If you've ever spent time around someone who doesn't wash you'll soon realise soap-dodging is no laughing matter.

So what are the main things someone your age should include in his morning routine?

● **Brush your teeth for two minutes (also before bedtime) and concentrate on your gum line (where your teeth join your gums).**
● **Floss your teeth.**
● **Rinse with mouthwash.**
● **Shower or have a bath every morning.**
● **Wash your face.**
● **Apply deodorant to your armpits.**

SHOPPING LIST

Toothbrush, preferably an electric one with a built-in timer.
Toothpaste
Dental Floss
Mouthwash
Shower gel
Shampoo
Deodorant

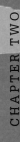

Brushing your teeth

Any dentist will tell you that the correct way to clean your teeth is to move the toothbrush in small concentric circles along the line where your gums meet your teeth. Make sure you **don't press too hard** as this can wear down your gums. Brush the front and the back of your teeth. Dentists recommend that you brush for **two minutes** each morning and night. Some electric toothbrushes have a built-in timer that will help you to brush for the correct amount of time.

Flossing

Flossing is just as important as brushing. When you eat, small particles of food can become **trapped between your teeth** and if you don't remove them they can rot. Think about tiny pieces of **rotten food** decaying against your gums and your teeth! There's no easier to way to make your mouth smell and seriously damage your dental hygiene. Floss before or after you brush to keep your teeth and gums healthy.

ZITS, BITS & STINKY PITS

24

Mouthwash

A fluoride mouthwash will help to strengthen your teeth against decay. Rinse your mouth with it for at least 30 seconds after brushing and then **spit it out**.

Washing & scrubbing

The way to wash or shower properly is to get a sponge or loofer and give your armpits a thorough scrubbing with some shower gel or soap. Once you're dry make sure you polish things off by applying some deodorant to your armpits. You'll be **looking** and **smelling good** and this will help you feel more self-confident, too.

Dear Alex,

Ever since I turned 12 I'm always really nervous around groups of people and in social situations. It's getting so bad that when my mates at school invite me out to the cinema I always make excuses so I don't have to face them. Every morning I look in the mirror and can't stand the person who looks back at me. I really need help to improve my confidence and make me feel better about the way I look so I can be around other people. Can you give me any practical tips that could help?

Tim, 12

Body confidence: quick fixes

It's hard to stay confident when every day your body seems to be trying to sabotage your appearance. Here are some quick fixes for those days when you look in the mirror and the end-of-level baddie from HALO stares back at you.

CONCEAL YOUR SPOTS

One of the main reasons you might be experiencing low self-esteem is spots: I've talked about what spots are and how to prevent them, but I realise that there will be days when you wake up to find they've taken over your face and you need an immediate solution.

You might think that makeup is just for girls, but there is a type called concealer that boys can wear (and do, in large numbers). Concealer is flesh-tinted makeup in a tube that looks like a lipstick. It's sold in pharmacies and comes in a range of different skin tones. You can keep a tube of it in your pocket and nip to the bathroom to cover up a spot as soon as it appears. The downside to concealer is that it's not great for your skin as it can block your pores. You need to wash it off every night before bed and only use it on a really bad day. Make sure you blend it in with your skin properly or everyone will be able to spot it (groan!).

WASH YOUR HAIR

Another reason you might be lacking in confidence is if you have greasy hair. It may sound obvious, but freshly-washed hair can make a big difference to your appearance. Lather, rinse, repeat and when you're done, dry it properly and comb or brush it into your preferred style.

If like Tim you are suffering from painful self-doubt, here are a couple of easy techniques you can use to build your confidence and boost your self-esteem:

CONFIDENCE REINFORCEMENT TECHNIQUES

When you feel the doubt kick in, repeat over and over in your mind **'I am cool and I'm as good as everyone else'**. You can change the words to suit whatever it is you have doubts about. I know it sounds corny, but it genuinely works. The more you tell yourself that you are confident the more you truly will feel confident. It's a technique I have been advocating in my columns for many years now and the feedback from my readers is extremely positive. One lad told me that it had completely changed his life and that eventually he couldn't believe that he had ever suffered from self-doubt in the first place.

WHAT DO YOU LIKE ABOUT YOURSELF?

When we look in the mirror we choose to centre our gaze on certain features. Confident people focus on the things they most like about themselves. There are tons of confident lads who are not typically 'handsome' or who may have bad acne but who go through life acting as if they're twins with Justin Bieber. What you may find surprising is that this approach works, because inner confidence outshines external appearance. It's about adjusting how you see yourself when you look in the mirror and focusing on the things you like about yourself. It's all a matter of perception. As the old saying goes, beauty is in the eye of the beholder! ❧

Healthy eating

A section on healthy eating you say? In a book you told me was going to be fun?

Well, yes, I'm afraid healthy eating gets its own section but for a very good reason. It may sound incredibly boring but healthy eating is how we get our **POWER-UPS**. Think of Super Mario eating that bonus mushroom! Eating properly will give you much-needed energy, while eating the wrong types of foods can make you overweight, tired and even worsen your spots!

Everyone knows the expression you are what you eat, but I wonder how seriously you take it. If you eat junk all the time your body can start to become mildly ill. Learning how to eat healthily not only prevents you from damaging your insides but can also stop you becoming unhealthily overweight or underweight.

A balanced diet

Health professionals such as doctors and health visitors advise us to eat a diet that balances starchy foods (such as rice and pasta) and foods that are rich in protein (such as meat, fish and lentils) with plenty of fruit and vegetables, some milk and dairy foods and smaller amounts of foods that are higher in fat, salt or sugar.

I know this is a lot of information to take in, but let's **break it down** so it's easier to understand.

Food falls into five basic groups. These are:

- Fruit and vegetables.
- Starchy foods (rice, pasta, bread, potatoes).
- Meat, fish, eggs, beans.
- Milk & dairy foods.
- Foods containing fat and sugar.

Fruit & veg

Fruit and vegetables are one of our **biggest** sources of vitamins and minerals. Without vitamins and minerals the human body stops functioning properly so they're one of the most important things we eat. You may have heard the expression **FIVE A DAY** as it's mentioned a lot in schools, at home and on TV. Eating five portions of fruit or vegetables a day has been proven to lower the risk of heart disease, stroke and some cancers — some of the worst illnesses or health problems you can get. It's got to be **worth** doing!

Starchy foods

Most of us eat a lot of starchy foods such as rice, pasta, bread and potatoes because they're **filling, tasty** and can be cooked or prepared in lots of different ways. The main building blocks of these foods are called 'carbohydrates' and they are a quick way for us to get energy. The problem with carbohydrates or 'carbs' is that we can only store a limited quantity of them. Once the body has reached saturation point it performs a clever trick. Abracadabra, hey presto, it **converts the carbs into fat**! So eating too many carbs can make you gain weight.

There's nothing wrong with putting on a few pounds but there's a difference between being a bit overweight and being obese. Obesity is a term that means 'very overweight' and it's a **DANGEROUS** condition. It can put immense pressure on your heart, damage your joints and cause diet-related illnesses such as diabetes.

Meat, fish, eggs & beans

These foods might seem to have little in common, but they all contain protein, another essential building block of the human body. Have you ever seen weight lifters or body builders in action? Lifting weights causes the fibres in their muscles to break down. Protein rebuilds their muscles and allows them to grow back **bigger** and **stronger**.

Protein is a **MUST** for all of us. It contains essential vitamins and minerals as well as giving the body what it needs to **grow** and **repair** itself.

Dairy foods

Dairy foods include cheese, milk, butter and yoghurt. Milk contains 'calcium' which is essential for strong healthy bones and teeth. Although dairy is an essential food group, it's important to think about how much fat dairy foods contain.

For example, cheese is high in fat and a piece the size of a matchbox contains enough energy to fuel an hour of hard walking. Think about that the next time you grate cheese on top of your spag bol – **sprinkle**, don't smother!

Milk can also be high in fat, but helpfully it comes in different varieties: full fat, semi skimmed and skimmed. As you might have guessed from the name, full-fat milk contains the most fat (about 3.5%). Semi-skimmed milk provides a good compromise between tasting nice and **being healthy**.

Butter is also full of fat but every spread and margarine contains fat too. It's best to try to ration your total intake – instead of saying: "Oh, I can eat tons of margarine because it's not butter!"

Fat & sugar

Both fat and sugar are **HIGH ENERGY** sources and the problem you have when you eat too many high-fat, sugary snacks is that your body is unable to make use of all that energy. Just like carbs, it converts the excess to fat and stores it in the body. If you want to **live a long life** and stay trim then it's easy – avoid eating too many sugar-laden and fat-filled foods.

It's also useful to know the difference between saturated and unsaturated fat. Foods like cheese, sausages, butter, cakes, biscuits and pies are high in saturated fat, which can raise levels of cholesterol in your blood and eventually cause heart disease. Unsaturated fats on the other hand can be healthy when eaten in small quantities. These are found in foods such as oily fish, nuts and seeds, olive oil and avocados.

Keep an eye on calories

A calorie is a unit of energy and it's a way to monitor **how much fuel** we put into our bodies. Each day a boy between 9 and 13 needs around 2200 calories. If you want to make sure you don't over-eat or under-eat it can be helpful to know how many calories you are taking in each day.

Check the label before you buy

Food packaging includes colour-coded labels that can show at a glance if the product has a high calorie, fat, sugar or salt content. Green means low calorie and low fat, orange is medium, and red is very high. Next time you go into a shop, try and spot this label on some of the products you see. You might discover that some foods, such as pre-packaged sandwiches, are less healthy than you think.

Exercise is for everybody

Usually boys your age fall into two groups, those who enjoy exercise and those who don't. A lot of the time this can be because you either love team sports such as football or you absolutely **hate** them.

I know it can be really difficult if you're not one of the sporty lads at school, but exercise doesn't have to be about impressing your teammates or scoring the winning goal. A mere 30 minutes of ANY form of exercise that gets your heart rate up and has you **sweating** at least twice a week will help build your muscles, burn calories and do wonders for your **self-esteem**.

You may also have avoided exercise in the past because at first it's really difficult to get going. You go red in the face, start to pant and your lungs feel like they're going to burn or **burst**. But that's only on the first couple of times. If you stick at it and get through those early sessions you'll soon find it gets easier and you'll start to feel REALLY BRILLIANT AFTERWARDS.

You don't need a gym membership or tons of expensive sports equipment to exercise. On the next page are some simple exercises you can do twice a week. They'll let you break a sweat and get the blood pumping through your heart (known as cardiovascular exercise or CV). This is the **best kind of exercise** for prolonging your life, and burning calories if you are trying to keep your weight down.

Exercise at no extra cost

Jogging

20 minutes of jogging at a moderate pace. It's tough at first but is one of the most effective ways to break a sweat.

Walking

While similar to jogging, walking is less intense and can be less painful if you're new to moving faster. Bear in mind you will have to walk for between 45 to 60 minutes to get the same benefit as you would from around 20 minutes of jogging.

Stair Steps

There are gyms filled with exercise equipment that mimic climbing stairs but why pay the big bucks when you can use the real thing? Find a building with a big set of stairs (such as your school) and simply walk or jog up and down them at a moderate pace. Stair steps can be tough after a while but are a great workout and really good on those leg muscles.

Squats

Ask your gym teacher at school to show you how to do these. They're a great lower body exercise that works out parts of all your major muscle groups and gets your blood pumping.

Pushups

Your gym teacher can show how to do these resistance-based exercises. They strengthen your arm muscles and if done properly will make you break a sweat. Start by doing only a handful and work your way up to whatever feels comfortable.

Situps

These are a form of exercise that are excellent at strengthening your stomach muscles.

Girls aren't aliens

(whatever you may think)

Dear Alex,

My mum said my sister has become a woman now because she had something called her period. They won't tell me what this is but I'm dying to know. Will I have a period too when it's time for me to grow up and become a man? If so, what will it look like?

Daniel, 9

If you know what a period is and know about girls' puberty then you might have found Daniel's question funny. Before you laugh too hard though, you should know that it's actually quite a common one. Lots of boys your age **DON'T** know much about girls' bodies and how they change.

I'm not going to go into too much detail about girls' puberty (there's more information in **THE GIRL FILES**), but I do want to clear up any confusion you may have about how it differs from that of boys.

The main differences

- **Girls begin puberty earlier than boys, on average by about two years.**
- Girls' puberty is driven by the hormone oestrogen, which has the effect of producing a female shape and organs.
- **Girls have periods. These can start at any age between eight and 16 years old, although more commonly around the age of 12. Once a month a tiny egg is released inside a girl's body and for part of that month the egg can be fertilised by a boy's sperm. When this doesn't happen the levels of female hormones in her body drop off and she sheds the lining of her womb in the form of a discharge with blood. It's perfectly natural and all girls do it. It does not happen to boys so Daniel did not need to worry.**
- Breasts. Girls start to develop breasts around the age of 11 (in some cases they can get breast 'buds' as early as eight).
- **It's worth adding that girls can have a difficult time during puberty as their bodies go through these huge changes, and they deserve your respect and understanding.**

Girls certainly aren't **aliens** and they don't come from another planet. In fact there are more similarities between boys and girls than there are differences.

In this section I want to share with you some problems that have been sent to me by girls your own age

"All the girls at school laughed at me yesterday because one of them said I smelled of BO. I didn't even know what it was until my mum told me."
Hannah, 9

"Since turning 12 I can't help but oversleep all the time. On the weekends I stay in bed until 12pm and I've been turning up late for school as well. My mum says it's all part of 'the change'."
Bernie, 12

"All the girls at school tell me they've started their already but I'm the only one who hasn't. I feel like I'm being left behind. Sometimes puberty feels like a race that I'm losing".
Anne, 13

"Since starting puberty I've gained almost half a stone in weight. I've turned into a fat spotty mess."
Shanti, 11

"I'm terrified of puberty. My mum has told me about all the changes that are going to happen and I just wish they wouldn't. I wish I could make it go away."
Leila, 10

to illustrate that they have the same worries and anxieties as you do. Hopefully once you realise the differences are mainly *surface deep* you'll have an easier time relating to girls in general.

Once you've read some of these problems you'll see that girls suffer all the same sorts of stuff as boys, and then some. Yes boys and girls have their differences, but we should treat girls with respect rather than as aliens from the **Planet Zarg**.

"The other day I got so mad with my mum and dad that I wouldn't speak to them all day. This is really unusual behaviour for me. I know it's the hormones but it doesn't help when I'm angry as it feels so real."
Phillipa, 13

"My best friend has bigger boobs than me. She already wears a grown-up bra and everything. I look in the mirror every morning hoping mine will grow more but they never do".
Michelle, 12

"Every morning I wake up I have a new zit right in the middle of my forehead. It's getting so bad I don't ever want to leave the house again. I wish puberty would just hurry up and be done with me!"
Amber, 11

"I'm bullied at school because I have hairy armpits. My mum says it's because I'm an early developer but that doesn't help when I'm being called names. It's so unfair!"
Karen, 10

"All the girls at school are at least a foot taller than me. I'm sick and tired of being the tiny one. When will I get my growth spurt?"
Samantha, 13

CHAPTER 4

owths, spurts, gorilla hair

and a voice like VADER!

Dear Alex,

I was reading aloud in class and all of a sudden it was as if I couldn't control my voice – it was squeaky one minute and growly the next. Everyone laughed at me but the teacher said it was normal for a boy my age. What was he talking about and how do I make it go back to the way it was?

Greg, 13

Breaking voices

Unless you've been **living in a cave** for your entire life
then you will have come across the deep booming voice of the
villainous Darth Vader in the Star Wars movies. You may also
have watched as his journey began as boy of about your age in
Episode 1: The Phantom Menace. But have you ever wondered
how that young man with his squeaky voice ended up sounding
like everyone's favourite Sith Lord? Like all teenage boys his voice
broke as puberty began.

How does it happen?

Like many of the other changes brought on by puberty your voice
breaking is triggered by testosterone. It all begins in a part of your
throat called the larynx, or voice box. Stretched across your larynx
are two very important muscles, your vocal chords. When you
speak air rushes from your lungs into your larynx and makes your
vocal chords **vibrate**. You learn to control this vibration as you
learn to talk.

Thinking of your vocal chords as if they were rubber bands is a
good way to understand how puberty goes about making your
voice deeper. Have you ever held a thin rubber band between
two fingers and given it a twang? The twanging noise it makes,

which is caused by vibration, is quite high-pitched. Now think about what happens when you twang a thick rubber band. The noise sounds a lot deeper. This is just what happens to your vocal chords during puberty.

During puberty your larynx gets bigger and your vocal chords become longer and thicker. Areas in your sinuses, nose and the back of your throat widen so that your new voice has more room to resonate. As your larynx grows you might notice the beginnings of a **bump in your throat** called an Adam's apple. It's only found in boys because their larynx grows that much bigger than girls'.

How will you know when your voice breaks?

The first sign you have that your voice is changing will be when you go to speak and find a strange croak comes out instead. Odd, you'll think to yourself. Let's try that again. Encouragingly, this time your voice might sound a bit deeper, only to crack into a high pitched squeak again. And this is when you realise your voice has broken.

Just like learning to talk, you have to teach yourself to use your vocal chords again. This can take some **serious practice** during which time your voice might sound a bit strange. Don't worry, you'll soon master your new equipment and everyone will get used to hearing your new voice.

If like Greg, your voice breaks somewhere public, just laugh it off. There's no shame in it no matter how silly you might sound. If your mates do give you stick for it, then more than likely it hasn't happened to them yet. Console yourself with the knowledge that it happens to everyone and they've got it all in store for them!

Dear Alex,

I was in the bath the other day and noticed I have hair growing above my penis and a bit under my arms. My dad said it's because I'm becoming a man but I'm scared I'll end up looking like a gorilla (like my dad does!).

Joshua, 11

If you're concerned you might end up looking like an extra from **Planet of the Apes** then you needn't worry. Although you will grow hair in completely new places you won't end up looking like a gorilla (although it can feel that way sometimes). Until now you've only had hair growing on top of your head and it can be a shock to find it appearing elsewhere. Like so much we've discussed so far, pubic hair and body hair grow at different rates depending on the person.

Pubic hair

Pubic hair grows around your penis in an area called the *pubic triangle*. It will start growing around the age of 11 and you'll notice a few short hairs at the base of your penis. They'll soon become more numerous and you'll quickly get used to having pubic hair.

Body and facial hair

Just when you've accepted that you now have hair around your penis those pesky **male hormones** take things one step further. Body hair appears under your arms and between your bum. Next you'll find hairs sprouting from your upper lip and sideburns will start to appear. From here it's a short step to growing hair around your nipples and finally you'll be able to grow a beard. Of course this all happens **gradually** and depending on your hormone levels can take many years, even until you're well into adulthood.

42

Now you know a bit about body hair I thought it might help if you read the accounts of some older boys. Hopefully their stories will allay any fears you have about turning into Chewbacca and show that everyone develops at different rates:

"I started getting pubic hair when I was 10 and a half. I guess I was what you would call a fast developer because by the time I was 17 I had thick hair all over my body. I even grow hair on my back and have to get my mum to help to remove it because I don't like the way it looks. It's not that big a deal and after a bit of waxing no one is any the wiser."

Rhys, 19

"I am a very light blonde and so although I've got pubic and armpit hair, it's very fine and I look almost hairless. I'm really happy this way because I don't think lots of hair would really suit me."

Guy, 17

"I started getting pubic hair at the age of 12. I have armpit hair and a bit of hair on my chest but I'm generally pretty smooth all over. I used to grow a 'moustache' until my sister said it was 'bumfluff' and didn't look good. That was embarrassing!"

Charlie, 18

"I developed late and didn't get any pubic hair until I was 14. By then everyone else in my class had started getting facial hair and I was really jealous."

Bebb, 19

Dear Alex,

I used to be the shortest boy in my class but since I turned 12 I haven't stopped growing. When I play rugby I barely fit in the scrum. In the school photo I was towering over all the other boys at my school. I know it's good to be big but I always feel like the odd one out. Am I always going to be like this?

Alan, 14

Alan is experiencing a **GROWTH SPURT**, a very descriptive and appropriate word for what happens during puberty, when boys can gain up to nine centimetres in a year. Growth spurts are caused by (you guessed it) testosterone, and they are one of the key experiences of puberty.

Growth spurts follow their own unusual logic and start from the outside in. Hands and feet grow first and can look disproportionate in relation to your body until the rest of it catches up. When your mum has to take you to buy three pairs of new school shoes in the space of a few months you'll know that puberty has well and truly set in.

Shortly after this your arms and legs follow suit. Your shin bones lengthen before your thighs do and your forearms before your upper arms. Your spine grows next and then your chest and shoulders broaden to complete the process. Remember at the beginning of the book when I said puberty would **transform you**? Well this is what I was referring to.

Balancing act

A side-effect of growing so quickly, and one that can take you by surprise, is that your brain can take a while to catch up with the new size and shape of your body. It's simply not used to having such long limbs. The result is that where once you were agile and nimble, suddenly you are **gangly** and **clumsy**. Just like breaking in your new vocal chords this all sorts itself out once you've learned how to use your new body.

45

Sleeping late

and controlling the HATE!

Dear Alex,

I used to love getting up early every Sunday morning to spend time with my little brother and watch cartoons with him. Last year I started to get pubic hair and had my first growth spurt. I grew five centimetres almost overnight. Now I'm finding it really hard to get up in the morning and I really miss my old routine. If I try to get up earlier I feel completely exhausted. How do other teenagers cope with the tiredness? I just wish I was less tired.

Martin, 15

From reading Martin's letter you'd be forgiven for assuming he had some kind of **sleeping sickness**. In reality it's not an illness that's causing him to need more sleep but his own body. Once again it's puberty's hormones doing their thing.

Sleep and puberty

The physical upheaval caused by puberty disrupts your body chemistry, particularly the part that tells you when you need to sleep and how long for. When the changes are at their most intense (between the ages of 13 and 17) insomnia is common. You might find yourself lying awake until 3am wishing you could **get some shut-eye**. When you do finally drop off, your body will stubbornly refuse to wake up until it's had much more than the usual eight hours. Teenagers can happily sleep until lunchtime and beyond.

One theory why teenagers need more sleep is that because the body is going through such DRASTIC CHANGE it needs to rest and recharge. Researchers have also suggested that the body clock gets displaced by an extra two hours, so that what feels late to most people seems much earlier to a teen. This would explain why it can be so hard for teenagers to get to sleep.

Interestingly, new research also suggests that it is sleep itself that is the trigger for the changes of puberty. Scientists think that the parts of the brain that control puberty are activated during **deep sleep**, producing our old friend testosterone. So not only can puberty create a form of sleep disorder, but problems with sleeping can slow down development.

47

Sleep solutions

In Chapter One I suggested that the solution to teenage tiredness was to get to bed a bit earlier. "Hold on", I hear you say, "didn't you just tell us that teenagers find it much harder to get an early night?" Yes I did, and this is a hard problem to solve. What can help is a proper bedtime routine that ensures you've wound down properly and one that means you are fast asleep as soon as your head hits the pillow. Here is a list of helpful suggestions:

Don't drink caffeinated drinks like cola or even tea directly before bed as these will keep you awake.

Avoid eating chocolate in the late afternoon or early evening. Chocolate contains a stimulant called theobromine that is very like caffeine in the ways it can affect you.

Cut down on sugar-rich foods directly before bed. Otherwise you'll find yourself wide awake with bags of energy.

Don't play electronic games, watch TV or use a computer at least an hour before going to bed. All computers and TV screens emit 'blue light' which has the effect of suppressing the production of melatonin, the hormone that makes us sleepy.

Make sure your room is completely dark and silent. You need to shut down your senses and stop stimulating your mind.

You're never too old for a bedtime companion, whether this is an old teddy or snuggling up with the cat. You might think it sounds silly but having something soft and comforting can really help you to drift off.

Dealing with feelings

My parents are SO embarrassing. Whenever we go out to the shops my dad has to do something to humiliate me. We'll be in the queue for the checkout in a supermarket and he'll start singing out loud. Everyone ends up looking at him and I cringe and go red. Other times he says stuff that's just awful. I can get really angry with him and we've had some terrible arguments. I can really lose control and once ended up almost hitting him.

It gets worse - he and my mum have been my friends on Facebook for ages, but now I find that really embarrassing and wish they weren't. They don't seem to realise that whilst Facebook is virtual the people on it are real and I have to show my face in front of everyone from school. It's really sad because my dad and I used to get on SO well.

Jamie, 15

There is some debate about the causes of teenage mood-swings, embarrassment, depression, anger and irritability. A likely explanation (but still an unproven one) is that the **rapid rise** in the levels of hormones like testosterone during puberty can make people's emotions go up and down like a yo-yo. This would certainly account for how out of character feelings like Jamie's can be.

There will be plenty of times when you'll feel fed up with the havoc puberty is wreaking on your body. Zits, oily skin and putting on weight are all things that might lower your self-esteem. If you are lacking in confidence, the last thing you want to do is leave your bedroom and present yourself to the outside world. Parents become an extension of yourself and their antics therefore seem **ten times more embarrassing** than before.

Embarrassment

Part of being a teenager is about becoming much more aware of the external world and its standards. As you start to be aware of how other people see things, or what is considered cool or trendy, you begin to judge everyone around you, but most of all you judge your mum and dad. Even if they were Hollywood movie stars there'd still be times when they'd make you feel like **hiding your head in shame**. This really isn't their fault. The problem lies in your self-confidence and it isn't going to go away until you start to feel better about yourself.

Keeping control

There are various strategies for coping with yo-yo feelings. The best one is often to **bite your tongue** and try not to overreact. If you feel your emotions bubbling up, take a deep breath and count to 20. If you're still really upset, try talking through your problems rather than exploding with anger. Your parents will respect a calm conversation a lot more than a tantrum and are more likely to take on board what you're saying.

The good news is, when you emerge from your teens into your twenties, things change. Your parents will still be the same people but somehow their faults and peculiarities will no longer seem so offensive to you. In fact you may start to love those unique behaviours which before you only saw as irritating.

In the meantime, try and realise that, despite how it may feel to you, **people don't confuse you with your parents**. If you want to be 'cool' then be 'cool' and let your parents be themselves.

One final piece of advice: if you want your private life to remain so, don't accept your mum and dad's friend requests on Facebook. Reassure them that you love them dearly but explain **you need your own space**, in the real world and online.

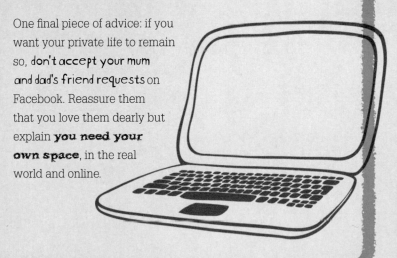

Social anxiety and feeling different

School can be a tough environment for a teen. Hormones can make you feel self-conscious about your body and the constant physical changes don't help. You start to *evaluate* how other people see you and **make judgements** about yourself: am I fatter than him? Am I too skinny? Can they see my spots? Is my willy as big as his? Am I the only boy who hasn't had a growth spurt? Am I the only boy who **HAS** had a growth spurt?

It's important not to upset yourself with constant self-evaluation. In a few years you and all your friends will be *unrecognisable* to each other from the way you look now, and your concerns about who has the most spots, the biggest willy or the squeakiest voice will no longer be relevant.

In the meantime, it's really important to try and talk through these **NORMAL** teenage anxieties with your mum or dad and don't keep them bottled up inside. The sooner you tell them when you're feeling low, the sooner they can help.

A recent study showed that one in eight children between nine and 17 suffer from social anxiety disorder, which is brought on by *low self-esteem* and causes **chronic shyness**. If someone is feeling very low, a doctor can refer them to see a councillor. It sounds scary but it just means they can talk about their problems with someone who will know *ways to make them feel* better.

Talking it through with your mum and dad

Having a good relationship with your parents makes it easier to talk things through with them when you feel down. They might make social boo-boos, embarrass you and provoke your anger but they are the best people to listen to you when you feel low. They may never be 'cool' but they can certainly be a **comfort** and will always have your best interests at heart, no matter how it sometimes feels. Even when your parents are being difficult and have really upset you, try and take it on the chin and remember that everyone makes mistakes. Your mum and dad aren't always perfect but they are your mum and dad and they love you very much.

Peer pressure

'Peer pressure' is when other boys and girls of your age (your peers) make you feel like you should be doing something you wouldn't normally do. This can be anything from wearing a certain fashion or listening to a type of **music**, to drinking alcohol or smoking a **cigarette**. You may not even realise you are under the influence of peer pressure because of how **POWERFUL** the impulse is to want to fit in. My advice is to think things through properly and make sure you know why you're doing something before you do it.

People do silly things because of peer pressure. It helps them to feel popular and **accepted**, and makes those feelings of social anxiety go away. It can also be the reason why many of us make some of the **worst decisions** of our lives. I'll talk more about this in Chapter 9.

CHAPTER 6

The wandering willy

Willy worries and unexpected erection

Dear Alex,

I was in swimming class with other boys from school and I got an erection. I was terrified they might see it and call me gay. More and more these days I feel like I no longer have control over my penis; it seems to have a life of its own. When I wake up in the morning it's always erect and will get hard at other times for absolutely no reason at all. It's really getting me down because I feel like I don't have control over my own body, and that feels scary.

Mark, 13

Until you hit puberty your willy doesn't feel very important. Its only purpose is to help you go to the loo. In the next few years the way you think about your penis is going to **change completely**. For a good while it's going to be one of the most important things in your life and the focus of plenty of agonising uncertainty as you get used to its new status.

Why do men get erections?

Men need erections so that when they're adults they can have sex. The penis gets rigid and very sensitive and can be placed inside a woman's vagina to transfer the sperm needed for making a baby.

Human beings have evolved over millions of years and throughout that time we have been shaped in our physical makeup by a process called natural selection. Over the aeons our ancestors would discover that a particular physical characteristic was favourable for **survival**. This meant that the individual who had this characteristic was more likely to reproduce. The offspring would also have the helpful characteristic, which in turn would increase their chances of passing it on. Fast-forward millions of years and there's you having an erection and wondering why it feels sensitive and can be **pleasurable to the touch**. The reason is simple; if it feels good to use your erect willy to have sex then the chances are you'll reproduce and make more little versions of yourself.

Of course, knowing **WHY** sexual arousal takes place is not going to help you to deal with the consequences.

Your first erection

The first time you have an erection you'll discover that your penis becomes a lot more sensitive than normal. Touching it can be **almost painful** at first but this hyper-sensitivity will decrease once you get used to it. The worst thing about erections is that you can get them anywhere at any time. It's true that thinking 'sexy' thoughts can be one way that they happen, but most of the time there won't be an obvious reason why.

You might have your first erection when you wake up one morning. You could be **on the bus** to school or at your gran's house watching a boring snooker match on the TV when all of a sudden you feel that familiar stiffness. In panic you'll be grabbing the nearest schoolbag or cushion to cover your lap until your unwanted visitor makes its exit.

Or, like Mark, you could get an erection when you're in the swimming pool with other lads. This does not mean you are gay, nor does mentally comparing your penis to that of other boys. If you were gay there'd be nothing wrong with that either, but having unexpected erections is not how you would find out.

The point is that your willy has **a mind of its own** and can get you into hot water if you don't learn some methods to 'tame' it. I'll discuss coping strategies in a moment, but first let's ask ourselves why we get embarrassed by erections.

Why do we get embarrassed by erections?

There are certain details of our lives that we consider **PRIVATE** and others that we are happy to **broadcast freely**. Erections fall into the private category. Bodily functions such as going to the toilet and sexual arousal are something society teaches us we should keep to ourselves.

This is for our own safety and because other people prefer not to be made aware of them.

It isn't because erections are unnatural, or because you are doing something wrong by having an erection, and it's important you understand this.

PRIVATE!

Classmates will always make fun of things they think are **forbidden** because they think talking about these subjects is 'naughty'. This is why keeping your erections to yourself when you're at school is a good idea. I agree that it's unfair that other boys might choose to laugh at something that happens to them too. Often the reason why will be their own fears of this kind of public humiliation. The logic might not make sense, but they are laughing at you because they're scared the same thing could happen to them.

Problem solved

Now I want to share with you some **willy worries** that have been sent in by lads your own age and the responses I gave to them. You might find the answer to one of your own problems here. If not then at least you can see how important our penises are and the sorts of things that can be cause for concern.

Dear Alex,

All the boys in my class have bigger willies than me. When we get changed for football the size difference is really obvious. I'm worried that something might be wrong with mine.

Tony, 13

There is no 'correct' size for a penis. We all develop at different rates and when our penises DO finish growing they each have their own shape and size. Some penises are long and thin, others are short and wide, some are small when soft but become much bigger when erect. The point is penis size is completely arbitrary – it means nothing! Bigger is not necessarily better. You are at the beginning of puberty and have a long way to go. Stop comparing yourself to other people – your penis will grow when it's ready and not before!

Dear Alex,

Help! I think I might have some kind of disease. I've noticed I get pimples on my willy and around its base. I know you can get diseases down there and they can be really bad. It doesn't hurt or anything but I am concerned.

Jason, 12

Ok, let me start by saying you are doing the right thing by keeping an eye on this sort of thing. You can breathe a big sigh of relief though, because the pimples you describe are quite common during puberty. Just like facial spots they are caused by extra oil secretions from your skin. They are just blocked pores that will clear up in time.

Dear Alex,

I was looking at myself in the mirror recently when I had an erection and I noticed that my penis hangs to one side and twists at the end. Is this normal or is there something wrong?

Andrew, 13

Your willy is perfectly normal. Like everything else in nature willies can be irregular in shape. They can hang to one side, have a twist at the end or even be slightly bent. You might also find you have one testicle that hangs lower than the other, or testicles of different sizes. None of this says anything about you as a person or will impair the function of your bits in any way.

Dear Alex,

I know this is going to sound quite unpleasant and I'm actually a bit embarrassed to be writing to \you about this. My problem is that my willy smells really bad all the time. I'm worried there might be something wrong with it. Is this something you've heard of before and is there anything that can be done about it?

Roland, 14

You're in luck, Roland, because I certainly have heard of it before; it's called 'NOT WASHING' and there is a very simple cure for it, which is to learn how to clean yourself properly. If you don't already bathe or shower every day then start doing so now. Use soap or shower gel and lather your entire body. Then gently scrub in all your crevices, around your penis and under your arms. Once the bacteria are scrubbed away the bad smell will go immediately.

Coping with unexpected erections

So, I promised you some tips on how to deal with the **nightmare scenario** of the unexpected erection. This can happen at the worst of times and you need a way to deal with it, but with all those teenage hormones raging through your body it's easier said than done. There is no way to prevent an unexpected erection happening, but there is a method of coping with it once it arrives.

First let me reassure you; when you have a public erection you imagine it's going to attract the attention of everyone around you. In reality though, there's almost no chance anyone will notice it, and even less chance they'd be crass enough to mention it or make an issue of it.

Your penis is influenced by your state of mind. While you don't have to think sexy thoughts to have an erection in the first place, a good way to get rid of one is to think about the **least sexy thing** you can imagine. Firm favourites over the years have been to think of your grandma telling a story, or picture yourself doing geography homework, or think about opening your Christmas presents. As long as you focus on something that is mundane and completely un-sexual, there's a very good chance your erection will subside.

This technique honestly works and I'm willing to bet it's been used at least once by every man who's been through puberty.

Staying safe

Emotionally, physically & online

Dear Alex,

Ever since I turned 15 I've been getting into a lot of trouble. When I get angry I see red and I lash out at people. I've been in tons of fights at school and punched one boy on the nose so hard it bled. My mum and dad were called into school by the headmaster to talk about my behaviour. When I get angry the feeling overwhelms me and I can't seem to stop myself. My mum says she's worried about my safety and that I can't go into the world thinking violence solves problems.

Barry, 15

THE BOY FILES wouldn't be complete without a chapter on safety. Learning about your body and how it's going to change is vital, but learning to stay safe is even more so. There are plenty of ways in which your new body and new emotions can get you into trouble. I'm going to look at three distinct areas of your life where being safety conscious is a **must**:

● **Emotional safety** – In this section I will talk about strategies for coping with extreme emotions like the ones Barry wrote to me about in the problem at the start of the chapter. I'll examine what sorts of events might lead to these types of outbursts and why it is essential to get your temper under control.

● **Street safety** – I'll give you practical tips on becoming street smart and on how to avoid potentially dangerous situations.

● **Cyber safety** – there are as many dangers in the virtual world as there are in the real one. I'll be giving sensible advice to make sure you stay safe online.

Emotional safety
Getting a handle on your anger

In Chapter 5 we looked at how **yo-yo feelings** might be a cause for concern, but now I want to look at what happens when your emotions get seriously out of control and become destructive.

Violence

When you feel powerless it might be tempting to lash out when things don't go your way. Most people learn that using violence is **not** how to resolve conflict and will end up damaging them more than anyone else. Violence can lead to someone being **excluded** from school and in trouble with the police, alarm their parents and drive away their mates. No one wants to be friends with someone who scares them and could hurt them at any moment.

Taking responsibility

The first step towards taking control of your anger is to take responsibility for it. No matter how much someone else may **wind you up, insult you, or make you jealous**, the person who is responsible for the violent reaction is going to be you. Words can be extremely hurtful but this doesn't mean you have the right to resort to violence.

Finding the cause

Identifying the 'triggers' that upset you is the next step towards **controlling your anger**. Triggers can be things like feeling misunderstood, disrespected, having expectations placed on you or when someone tells you 'no'. Once you can recognise what the triggers are you can defuse the **extreme emotions** they lead to.

SOLVE IT!

Take evasive action

When you get really angry it can be like a red mist descending across your vision. Pay attention the next time you fly off the handle and you'll notice there are **physical sensations that come hand in hand with the strong emotional reaction**. Your heart rate will increase and you'll get what is called an adrenaline rush. Adrenaline is a hormone that is released during times of extreme stress.

Feeling that first rush of adrenaline is an **early warning sign** that the red mist is about to descend. If you feel like a situation could provoke you to violence, as soon as you feel the adrenaline **make a swift exit**. Walk away. Avoidance will always be a better solution than violence. Once you've calmed down you'll be really proud that you had the strength to walk away.

Another thing you can do, as soon as you feel that first rush of adrenaline, is to repeat to yourself "**things are going to be ok, I can still be upset and not hit someone**". If it sounds corny then you haven't tried it. Talking yourself round is a proven and effective method of dealing with lots of challenging and frightening situations.

SOLVE IT!

Learn to prevent your anger

If you have a lot of anger inside you, you probably have very good reasons for feeling it. Life isn't always fair and can leave many of us with a lot of pain to deal with. One way to prevent violent conflicts from flaring up is to isolate what it is at the root of your dissatisfaction and talk about it with a professional. Visiting a counsellor or therapist (essentially the same thing) is nothing to be scared of. Their job is to give you some private space to get things off your chest.

A counsellor might help you see there are lots of coping exercises you can do. These can be activities such as 'taking a timeout' and sorting the problem later, exercising, listening to soothing music or taking deep breaths. It can also help to keep a journal of your thoughts and write down the things that upset you. Seeing your feelings on the page is amazingly therapeutic and can bring you the inner peace you need.

There are lots of counselling organisations that offer services for young people. A good place to begin would be to talk the idea through with your mum or dad and show them the list of helpful links on pages 94 and 95 of this book.

Staying safe on the street

In the next few years, your mum and dad will start to give you more independence. As a young teen you can do all sorts of cool things that you couldn't before.

You'll be able to:

- **Walk to school by yourself.**

- **Go to the movies and see the latest Spiderman film without an escort.**

- **Meet up with your mates and munch on pizza.**

- **Plan your own travel and take buses and trains on your own or with friends.**

This independence comes with a price, which is that you have to take responsibility for yourself instead of relying on someone else.

Here are some tips to help you to stay safe and keep out of trouble when you're out and about:

● **Tell people where you are going – or leave a note.**

● Keep your mobile phone charged up with your mum and dad's numbers programmed into it. Make sure you know the route back to where you live and your home address.

● **Stay alert when you're walking along the street. Switch off your MP3 player so you can hear what's going on around you. Pay attention to traffic, particularly when you want to cross the road, and anyone you don't know that gets close to you.**

● If you think someone might be following you cross the road and find somewhere with lots of people, like a shop or a bus stop.

● **Don't look strangers in the eye. Some people get upset or react aggressively to eye contact and it can provoke a 'situation'.**

● Stick to busy, well-lit main roads and avoid taking short cuts down dark side streets or alleys.

● **If you are going to take the bus, get off at a stop along a well-lit section of road, preferably with people around.**

● If someone does stop you or tries to 'mug' you, don't think it's smart to fight back. If they demand your phone or cash, give them up. Phones and money are easy to replace. Your life or health aren't.

● **Keep your valuables out of sight at all times.**

● Never carry any kind of weapon as this is more likely to be used against you than help you in a fight.

● **Shout for help and make a noise if you are being followed. This is more likely to scare away an attacker.**

Cyber safety: a user's guide

As I'm in my thirties I can remember what life was like before the web, but for you it's always been there, like TV has for me. When I was growing up people used to demonize TV, saying "watching too much telly will give you square eyes", "TV is dumbing down the youth of today", and "TV promotes violence and swearing".

In the internet age a similar trend has taken place, and using the social media sites can be made out to be more dangerous than it actually is. In reality as long as you stick to a few very important rules you should be fine.

Safety tips for smart surfing

- **The Internet is forever! You can't take back the things you write or the images you post. Even if you delete them the chances are someone else may have read them, screen captured them or saved them. Don't write or post anything that you might regret or that could get you into trouble.**

- Keep the settings on your social media accounts set to 'private' so only those people you give permission to can read your posts.

- **Don't give out your address, phone number or any other personal information about yourself. In chat rooms never use your real name or leave hints as to where you might live or places you visit.**

- Never agree to meet anyone you've met online in the real world. Take this warning very seriously, it's the most important rule of all.

CHAPTER SEVEN

69

- Remember, people online aren't always what they seem. Anyone can post a picture and write some text. It doesn't mean they are who they say they are. Keep your identity in chat rooms secret and use a different 'handle' or 'screen-name' to the one you use for Facebook and Twitter.

- Never accept unsolicited SKYPE calls or MSN webcam links. These could be anyone and you might not like what you see.

- **Don't add people you don't know on MSN – this reveals your Microsoft ID to the person and they will know when you login, have links to your X-Box Live account and be able to email you.**

- If someone you don't know adds you on Facebook be suspicious. Social networking is great and it is possible to meet new people online but it's best to do this through mutual friends. Don't make friends with random strangers as you have no idea what they're capable of.

- **Always log out of your Facebook and Twitter accounts when you use a public computer (like at school). Make sure your phone has a pin number so it can't be used by anyone else. If someone gets access to your accounts they can assume your identity and make a complete mess of your life.**

- Remember the Internet may be 'virtual' but it's not a game. When you use social networking sites the same rules of conduct apply as in real life. After the London riots many rioters were jailed for the things they wrote on social media sites. Status updates are a serious business!

- **If someone gives you abuse online, don't rise to the bait. Some of the more unsavoury characters you'll meet online enjoy a pastime called 'trolling'. They deliberately try to make you angry by saying things to upset you. They might post on your Facebook profile (if you were careless enough to accept their friend request) and say horrible, personally insulting things. It could also happen in a chat room. For example, a troll might visit a chat room for devout Christians and post remarks** claiming there is no God and insulting people's beliefs. Such trolls are looking for a reaction so it's best not to give them one.

● Think carefully when you're creating a new email address. Use something unconnected with your real name with a combination of letters and numbers. The more clues you leave for hackers to break into your account, the easier you make it.

● **If you begin an online friendship with someone, even if you meet them through mutual friends, be alert for any inconsistencies in what they tell you. If you are ever daft enough to break the golden rule and meet someone in RL (real life) that you've befriended online, please don't do it without letting your mum and dad know exactly where you are going and who you intend to see, and take a friend with you.**

● Treat people in online games with the same caution you would in a chat room – there is no difference at all!

CHAPTER 8

Bullying is a dirty word

So speak up and be heard!

Dear Alex,

There is a gang of boys at school who are making my life a misery. They push me around all day and threaten me. They're always telling me that I'm worthless and making personal remarks about me. One of them managed to hack into my Facebook account by stealing my phone and changed all my photos to rude pictures. He left statuses insulting all my friends and family and saying other things too rude to print. It's getting so bad that I no longer want to go to school. I don't feel at all safe there and just wish I could be left alone in my room. I thought about telling a teacher but one of the boys told me they'd follow me after school and beat me up if I did and that the teacher wouldn't be there to stop them. Please help!

Matthew, 12

Who gets bullied?

We all get bullied at some point in our lives. It can be by our parents, brothers and sisters, our friends or even by a teacher or other adult.

Whose fault is it?

Bullying is NEVER your fault, no matter what the bully tells you or how you're made to feel. Bullies look for victims and can be quite merciless when they have someone in their power.

Laughing along with a bully

Bullies will often pick on members of their social group, like their class at school. The bully might hit someone or threaten them, or he might try and make them believe horrible things about themselves to destroy their self-esteem. This often happens in front of lots of other members of the group and nine times out of 10 they'll laugh along – because they find it funny or because they are scared the bully will start picking on them.

What's worse, the boy who hits someone or the 20 others who laugh, and make the victim feel like the bully has the support of the whole group? They might not have been the ones to instigate the attack but by laughing they are supporting it and joining in as well.

Next time someone in your group gets bullied don't laugh along. Try and stop others from doing so as well. If the group stops supporting the bully he'll soon stop seeking its approval and leave the target of his bullying in peace.

A serious business

I don't want to scare you but I do want to make clear that bullying can have terrible consequences. Being the target of bullying can completely destroy a person's confidence. It can leave them feeling uncertain and nervous socially, and unable to be comfortable in or around groups. In extreme cases it can lead to suicide.

If you think someone in your school is being bullied, speak up and be heard. Tell a teacher or even your parents and ask them to take it up with the school. Do the right thing. It's better to be called a snitch than know that your lack of action means an innocent victim feels desperate. Your school should have an anti-bullying system in place that can deal with the problem. Even if your school ignores the bullying, don't give up. Keep pushing until you're sure it's being taken seriously.

How to handle a bully

● **If you're being bullied, tell one of your mates what is happening to you. It's harder to pick on two people than one.**

● Say NO! If a bully tries to get your attention or interact with you in any way just say a firm 'NO' and walk away. If you aren't prepared to be bullied you make the bully's job a lot harder.

● **Don't beg to be left alone – the bully wants you to get upset and behave like a victim and for the group to laugh along. If you deprive them of the satisfaction they'll give up and look elsewhere for their kicks.**

● Don't get into a fist fight. By their nature bullies like to pick on those weaker than themselves. This usually means they are bigger and stronger than those they target. By fighting them you are putting yourself at risk and you could end up getting blamed for the problem. Leave a clear line between who is the violent bully and who is being targeted.

● **Try saying 'Can you repeat that?' By asking a bully to repeat the nasty thing they said you are non-physically challenging them. Some bullies will find it harder to repeat the insult a second time – and even if they do it shows you are taking charge of the situation.**

● Prepare a snappy comeback. It's a lot harder to intimidate someone who has a prepared response, particularly if it's humorous. Bullies are cowards who pick on those who they consider weaker to make themselves feel important. What a colossal waste of time. By showing you have your wits about you there's a good chance they'll see you as an equal match and leave you alone.

● **Keep a diary or record of the incidents. If you keep track of all the times the bully threatens you or assaults you, you'll have a record in black and white that you can refer back to if you decide to speak to someone about it.**

Cyber bullying: what's it all about?

Cyber bullying is where a child or a teen gets harassed, threatened and humiliated by another child or teen online. If it were adults doing the same thing we'd call it cyber harassment and request it be investigated by the police.

How does it work?

Cyber bullying is carried out through whatever online technology the bully chooses. Often the website, application or game chosen just happens to be whatever the bully is interested in at that moment, rather than a deliberate tool to get to their victim.

Unlike real-life bullying, cyber bullying can go both ways, and the victim can strike back at the bully through similar channels and reverse the roles. This doesn't lessen the seriousness of the activity. In extreme real-life cases teens have killed one another and committed suicide following cyber bullying.

Instant messaging

Instant messaging is the most prevalent method of cyber bullying. Because so many programmes and technologies allow messaging there's no way for parents to 'police' the content their children are exposed to. The bullying can take the form of dozens if not hundreds of instant messages saying horrible things about someone. They can be threats to their safety or personal remarks that bring about serious depression and low self-esteem. They can be picture or video messages that are threatening or obscene. If you are receiving bullying messages and it's upsetting you report it immediately to your mum or dad or another responsible adult.

Account hacking

Account hacking is when someone deliberately hacks into one of your social networking or email accounts (or even gaming accounts) with the intention of doing as much damage as possible before you can change your password. I've already mentioned how important it is not to leave passwords lying around and for these to be strong to begin with.

Account hacking can lead to the bully replacing your

photos with obscene ones, or changing your personal information to nasty comments. The bully might also pretend to be you and cause damage to your relationship with friends or family who don't know what's happening.

Blog attack

Blogs are a public log of your thoughts and feelings. They are often quite intimate and because of this are usually shown only to friends and family. A cyber bully can hack into a blog (again by guessing or stealing a password) and write posts that damage the blogger's reputation. While it's possible to correct some of the remarks the damage may already have been done – making readers believe things about the blogger that are untrue.

Malicious websites

An elaborately vicious method of cyber bullying is to create a website attacking someone. One girl who wrote to my column had been the subject of such an attack and was pulling her hair out with the stress. Getting these types of sites taken down is really hard work. In the meantime the effect they have on the victim, knowing that people are visiting the site and reading the false, unpleasant comments, is extremely distressing.

Many phones come equipped with high-resolution cameras and the potential for their misuse by cyber bullies is obvious. The bully takes an intimate and unauthorised photo, in the school changing rooms for instance, and then sends this via a messenger app to a chosen group of others. Just like with physical bullying the target is horribly embarrassed while the group laugh along. It has been known for bullies to post images to peer-to-peer file sharing applications. Once images are on these networks it is impossible to remove them. From here they can easily get into the hands of sinister people who potentially could use them for anything.

Be vigilant

It is impossible to prevent the abuse and misuse of technology by cyber bullies, so it's super important YOU remain vigilant, safeguard passwords and only post pictures you're happy for people to see.

If things get really serious then you can go to the police although it's entirely possible they too will be limited in what steps they can take. Here are some tips on how best to deal with cyber bullying:

- Don't get drawn into it. It might be tempting to respond to your bully but doing so can easily make things worse.

- Delete any hacked accounts and change all your passwords.

- Never leave your phone, laptop or tablet unlocked.

- Don't share a photo unless you are happy for it to be seen by EVERYONE.

- Tell an adult you trust if you think you're being bullied.

CHAPTER 9

It's my life too

Coping with change

Dear Alex,

I HATE my mum and dad. Why do they think they have the right to tell me what to do? They always treat me like I'm a little kid. They insist on a really strict curfew. I have to be in bed asleep by 9pm. It's so unfair! All my friends are out having fun and meeting up when I'm lying wide awake in bed bored out of my eyeballs. I want them to realise I'm not a child anymore.

Archie, 13

I've included Archie's letter because it's a good example of something that most teenagers start to feel once puberty develops. As you grow more independent and start making your own decisions you may begin to question why you still need to follow the rules laid down by your parents.

The answer is simple. By law your parents are responsible for you until you turn 18. They are the ones who will get into the most serious trouble for the things that YOU do while you are defined as a child by law. I realise this doesn't help you much when you feel that their rules are unfair or that they don't understand you. I can see that it is hard, for example, if all your friends are allowed out on a school night and you're not.

Learn to negotiate

The key to getting your own way is not to make angry demands and expect them to be met. Present your argument in a calm and collected manner. Negotiate – and be prepared to compromise. This means giving up part of what you want if your parents will give up part of what they want – but to be able to negotiate properly you need to stay calm. If after you've explained your argument you still don't get your own way, you need to learn to accept it. You are going to have to live with the decisions your parents make (at least for now), and no matter how much they might get on your nerves, they deserve your respect.

Changing schools

Dear Alex,

I am 11 years old and have just started secondary school. I'm really nervous because I left all my friends behind at my old school and now I don't know anyone. I loved my school before and things were going really well for me. It seems like my life is over and I'm getting sucked into a black hole. My mum says my new school will be fine and it's no big deal but she's not the one who has to start all over again and not know anyone.

Peter, 11

Leaving primary school can seem really scary. Peter is not the only boy to be nervous about the future. I want to show that you can turn a negative into a positive and see starting a new school as a fantastic opportunity.

Here are some things you can do to make sure you get off to a good start:

● **During the summer before you start secondary school, think about what you'd like to change and what things about yourself you want to bring into your new environment.**

- Think about the kinds of friends you want to have at your new school and practise having fun conversations.

- **Now's the time to change the way you dress and choose a new, more grown-up image. Ask your parents to take you clothes shopping.**

- Make sure you follow a good bathroom routine (see page 23) – scrub yourself clean every morning and wear deodorant.

- **Finally get your new sleeping pattern into place before the term begins. As the new school year progresses you'll need more and more sleep. If you go to bed earlier you're more likely to wake up refreshed. It's hard to start a new school when you're half asleep.**

- Most important of all, don't worry! Things will turn out fine. This really is the start of a new chapter in your life and the adventure is only just beginning.

Breaking the rules

As we reach the end of The Boy Files I want to leave you with some cautions. There are actions and behaviours that you might be encouraged to participate in as you become a teenager which could land you in hot water. It's up to you to inform yourself in advance and choose to say 'NO!' to these.

Under-age drinking & smoking

These are both bad decisions. Drinking alcohol, particularly when you're under-age, leaves you vulnerable and out of control (not to mention it's illegal). If you get drunk you're likely to be very sick and in extreme cases could end up in hospital having your stomach pumped. There is nothing worse. You'll feel like you want to die.

Apart from smoking, of course. That's worse. Not only is it addictive, smelly and expensive, it gives you all sorts of health problems, including heart disease, and increases your chances of developing lung cancer ten times.

No matter how hard you try and avoid the temptation to drink or smoke there will always be other boys and girls doing it. You have to be strong when they encourage you to join them and say a very clear 'no'.

Vandalism

Vandalism, or deliberately causing damage to public property, is illegal and the police can arrest people for it. Vandals do it because they think it's clever and it gives them a temporary sensation of power. In reality it's stupid, shameful behaviour that makes them look like idiots.

Shoplifting

You might hear that it's easy to take small items from shops by slipping them into your pocket. Shoplifting is stealing and it's against the law. Almost all shops are equipped with cameras, mirrors and security guards who are on the alert for would-be shoplifters. Shop staff won't think twice about calling the police and having you arrested if they catch you stealing something. Shoplifting can be addictive and lead to someone becoming a repeat offender. The more they steal the more they want to steal – until they get caught. It's as simple as that.

Graffiti

There are different types of graffiti – some can be a form of art and look fantastic. The artist known as Banksy has become famous for his thought provoking images and designs. The key issue here is not about drawing on walls but whether you have permission to do it.

There's a massive difference between producing a piece of art with the permission of the person who owns the wall and spraying illegible 'tags', the ugly scrawls you see on the sides of buses and trains. Unfortunately this is the more common form of graffiti and possibly the kind your so-called friends will encourage you to attempt. The idea is that by 'tagging' something you are 'marking it' as your own. Huh! People won't know or care who's done the graffiti. Tagging is vandalism and people who are caught doing it will be arrested and possibly fined. At the very least they'll be made to spend hours cleaning off the mess.

Gangs

Some boys in secondary school become part of a gang. It might start out as a group of mates having a laugh and of course, if they're not hurting anyone, there's nothing wrong with that. Problems occur when the group realises that as a team they can get up to no good. Gang members can egg each other on to do stupid things and be aggressive towards others.

Gangs are the worst examples of peer pressure you'll come across. If you join a gang, you may be encouraged to leave graffiti tags on property, or to drink and smoke when you're under-age. You may be introduced to dangerous illegal drugs. If you want to stay safe, make sure you choose REAL friends over gang members who you have to take risks to impress.

Playing on train tracks

Many graffiti taggers and gang members are under the mistaken impression that it's cool to muck about on train tracks. Not only is it an illegal activity, it's a potentially fatal one. They may think they're being daring, but in reality they're risking their lives for nothing.

If you thought the other behaviours I've mentioned were dangerous, this is the worst. Some trains can move at well over 120 miles an hour. You try jumping out of the way of something going at that speed. Some train tracks have a 'live rail' with thousands of volts of electricity running through it at all times. One touch of this rail will deliver a fatal electric shock.

Real-life stories

To reinforce the cautions I've given you, here are four real-life interviews with older boys who lived to regret taking one risk too many.

"When I turned 14 I joined a gang at my school. Pretty soon we were bunking off most days and getting up to no good. At first it just seemed like lots of fun. My school work suffered and I got in trouble with my parents and teachers for not going but I didn't care. I was having the time of my life and nothing else mattered. Then one day we all thought it would be a great idea to break into the closed section of the nearby railway. We used to be into tagging and doing graffiti. I did a big 'piece' (a large tag) on the station wall. One of the other boys wanted to outdo me and so thought he'd be clever and drop down onto the tracks so he could tag the untouched wall on the other side.

I'll never forget that day. He stood on the live rail on his way across. One minute he was standing there and the next he'd collapsed. I had to give evidence at the inquest and his parents blamed me and my friends. I've never been the same since. Every time I close my eyes I can see him falling down. I went back to school and got my GCSEs but I wish I'd learned my lesson the easy way... by not joining a gang in the first place."

Larry, 18

"I started smoking when I was 12. All the other boys at school did it, or said they did at least. At first I'd nick my mum's fags from her bag. I was really into football when I was younger but the more I smoked the less I could run – I got too out of breath. So I stopped and just hung around with my mates. We used to smoke a lot. It's been five years now and I can't give up. I've tried a few times but it's impossible. I never have any money because I spend it all on fags and I'm fed up with smelling like an ashtray. I asked a girl out who I really fancied but she said no because of my 'fag breath'. I just wish I'd never started smoking."

Steve, 17

"I got obsessed with tagging at the start of secondary school. It was the cool thing to do in my group of friends. We all had our own tags and on the bus to school we'd tag every seat back, every wall and sometimes even scratch our tags onto the windows. My best friend wanted to be the one whose tag was most visible and ended up writing it all over the school. The teachers had a meeting and decided to exclude him. It was a big shock – it could have been me. I haven't tagged since that day. Looking back I realise how stupid it was. What did we get out of it? Absolutely nothing."

Jessie, 18

"My dad was a drinker. He used to come home drunk in the evening and was horrible to me and my mum. I swore I'd never end up the same way; I'd never drink. That's why it was so strange when I started. Me and the gang would meet up in this graveyard and all get completely wasted on strong lager we'd nicked from the local supermarket. For some reason I didn't think about my dad and what drink had done to him, all I thought about was getting off my face. I'm 25 now and have never had a job. I drink every day as soon as I get up. My doctor's told me that if I continue like this my liver will fail and I'll die. I want help so badly but I can't stop drinking. I never thought this would happen to me."

Lewis, 25

Lesson to be learned

I'm sure you'll agree that it makes you feel sad to read through these personal accounts of four people who have suffered because of the poor decisions they made in life.

Whilst not everyone who behaves like them will end up like them, the message is that participating in these types of high-risk behaviours is a gamble, and one that is easy to lose. Some people come through unscathed but many more don't. The sensible thing is to resist the pressure from "friends" to take risks you don't fancy. You only get one life. You are allowed to make mistakes. But big mistakes come with big price tags.

Live long & prosper

The accounts on the last few pages were there to show you what happens when poor decisions make things go wrong, but I don't want to end **The Boy Files** on a downer. Puberty is a fascinating journey and you're going to look back when it's all over and wonder at all the things that have changed – like a superhero coming into his powers. Very soon you'll be getting the first of these changes but hopefully now you'll feel more prepared and positive about what's in store.

Although I'm 20 years older than you, I still look back at my own journey through puberty and think of when I got my own powers. One I worked hard for was to have skill with words, so that I could become an author and write the very book you are holding. Writing this book has also made me think about the mistakes I made when I was growing up, and I've tried to share with you the things it cost me a lot to find out.

I don't want to tell you who to be or what to do. You're becoming a man now and you need to work hard over the next few years to learn to look after yourself and take responsibility for your actions. Remember:

● **If you skip school and slack off, the only person you hurt in the end is yourself. Don't let yourself be bullied and say 'no' when you're put under pressure. Speak up for yourself when the time is right and keep your thoughts to yourself when it's not.**

● **If you're having body confidence issues, look back at the techniques I've given you to deal with them. Use them to boost your self-esteem. No matter what anyone else says, you're just as important as everyone else on the planet and beauty is in the eye of the beholder.**

● If you don't understand something, ask for explanations and answers. Don't give up on anything you care about. Fight for what you believe in. Grab every opportunity that comes your way and don't ever say 'no' to something that could open up a new and positive pathway in your life.

● And be nice to Mum and Dad. They're the only parents you're going to get and I'm sure they love you very much. Hopefully, if you're nice to them they'll be nice to you!

Useful words

ACNE Or spots, pimples, zits. Caused by overactive sebaceous glands which make the pores clog up and become infected.

ANXIETY Feelings of fear, nervousness and stress, caused by people expecting too much of you, or by bullies, or even by you setting yourself too great a challenge.

DENTAL FLOSS A thin, tough, string-like substance sold in pharmacies and used for removing food trapped in your teeth which might otherwise rot and make your breath smell bad.

ERECTION Also known as a 'stiffie', this refers to the aroused condition of a penis when it becomes straighter and harder.

GENITALS The sexual organs. For a boy this means specifically the penis and testicles, for a girl the labia and vagina.

HORMONES Chemical substances that the body naturally produces. Hormones trigger the onset of puberty, the process which starts a child's transformation into an adult.

INSOMNIA The inability to sleep.

LARYNX The area at the back of the throat that houses the vocal chords.

MUSCLES The strong elastic tissue or sinews that hold the bones of the skeleton together.

OESTROGEN This is best known as the female hormone although boys have some of it too. But it is in girls that it has most effect. It is responsible for soft smooth skin, soft hair, and the development of girls' puberty.

PEERS Your peers are your friends, your own particular group, the people you grow up with, mates from school and those you want to impress. Peer pressure is the expectation that (you feel) these others have of you. What your friends think or want tends to shape your own behaviour even if sometimes, you don't like it.

PERIOD Another word for 'menstruation', the process that happens to girls every month when an unfertilised egg and the lining of the womb flow out of the vagina.

PUBIC HAIR This is the hair that grows around the genitals in the lead up to and during puberty.

SCROTUM This is the skin sack that hangs between your legs and contains your testicles.

SEBUM This is a greasy substance naturally secreted by the body and sometimes responsible for clogging up the pores and creating spots.

SOCIAL ANXIETY DISORDER Feelings of intense fear in social situations and worry about being judged by others and of being embarrassed or humiliated.

TESTOSTERONE Commonly known as the male hormone, although in fact both men and women possess it. Males have far more of it than females and during puberty boys are saturated with huge amounts of it.

TESTICLES Also known as 'balls'. Small round objects that hang in a sac between your legs and, as you grow up, begin to contain the sperm responsible for the boy's part in baby-making.

TROLL A person who is deliberately offensive online and who visits chatrooms and forums with the sole intention of upsetting people.

VAGINA Where boys have a penis, girls have a vagina. Instead of jutting out, like a penis, a vagina disappears inside a girl's body. This means that a penis can fit inside a vagina and not the other way round.

WET DREAMS This is an ejaculation during sleep that may well happen when you reach puberty (and later).

Get connected

Here are some helpful websites and groups specifically for young people.

BEAT BULLYING
http://www.beatbullying.org/
Says it's "the UK's leading bullying prevention charity, creating a world where bullying, violence and harassment are unacceptable. Beatbullying empowers people to understand, recognise, and say no to bullying, violence and harassment by giving them the tools to transform their lives and the lives of their peers. Working with families, schools, and communities to understand the problem, campaign for change and provide a sustainable efficient and proven solution".

CYBERMENTORS
http://www.beatbullying.org/dox/what-we-do/cybermentors.html
Online chat space called CYBERMENTORS where you can discuss bullying and get help from others who have faced the same problems. Offers help from people your own age.

CHILDLINE
http://www.childline.org.uk
Says it's for every child: "You can contact ChildLine about anything – no problem is too big or too small. If you're feeling worried, scared, stressed or just want to talk to someone you can contact ChildLine. We're here to offer information and support whenever you need us". Childline is there for any young person to call who's in trouble, facing a family problem, being abused or tormented. The service is free and confidential. Just ring 0800 1111.

GET CONNECTED
http://www.getconnected.org.uk/
Says it's "the free helpline for these young people, who know they need help but don't know where to find it. They can talk to us by phone, email and webchat any day of the year. Our Helpline Volunteers are fully trained to support each young person in their unique situation, and help them choose the best service from over 13,000 in the UK. Get Connected is the vital gateway between a distressing, confusing problem the young

person can't solve on their own and the service that can help them solve it. Crucially, the connection we make for each young person to their chosen source of help is free as well".

IT'S GOOD TO TALK
http://www.itsgoodtotalk.org.uk
A great website for connecting you with a counsellor in your area. Link through to the British Association of Counsellors and Psychotherapists. Has useful content such as 'What is Therapy?' and a search engine for the types of problems that therapy can be used to treat.

KIDSCAPE
http://www.kidscape.org.uk/
Says it's: "here to prevent bullying and child sexual abuse. Kidscape believes that protecting children from harm is key. Kidscape works UK-wide to provide individuals and organisations with practical skills and resources necessary to keep children safe from harm. The Kidscape staff equips vulnerable children with practical non-threatening knowledge and skills in how to keep themselves safe and reduce the likelihood of future harm" The helpline number is 08451 205 204.

KIDS' HEALTH
http://kidshealth.org/kid/
Special site to answer all your health questions in confidence – whether about illness or how you're feeling in general. Says it's offering: "information you can trust about kids and teens that's free of 'doctor speak'."

NHS PUBERTY INFORMATION
http://www.nhs.uk/Livewell/puberty/Pages/Pubertyinfoforchildren. aspx
Offers lots of info about growing up (including what's happening to girls). Loads of weblinks too.

THINK YOU KNOW?
http://www.thinkuknow.co.uk/
Another special site to help your age group stay safe, whether in daily life or while on the Internet.

Index